I REBUKE YOU DEVIL

I Am A Girl

By

Acillen K. Watts

I Rebuke You Devil, I Am A Girl

I Am
JOHN 3:16
Loved

God blessed woman to give birth to male or female children.

Female babies are girls and male babies are boys.

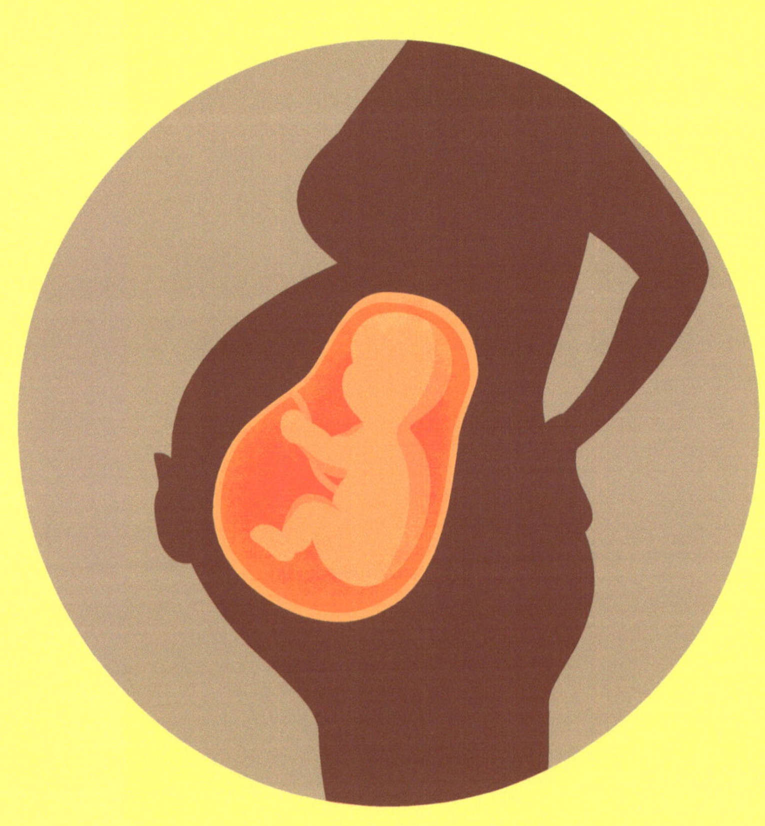

God loves the little children.
(Psalm 127:3)

Male and female he created them, and he blessed them and named them Man.
(Genesis 5:2)

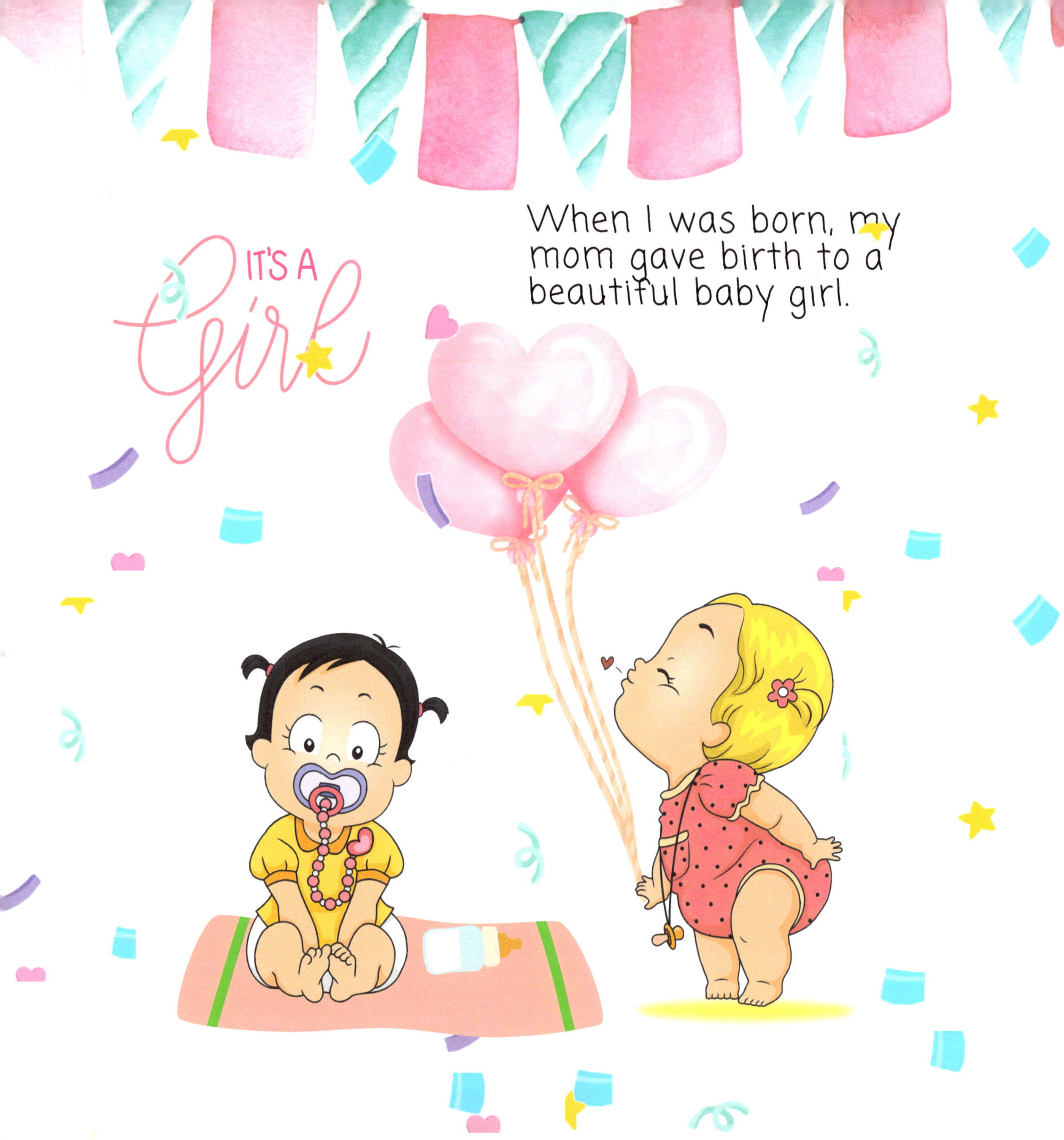
IT'S A Girl
When I was born, my mom gave birth to a beautiful baby girl.

Boys are not girls and girls are not boys.
(Numbers 23:19)

You are either a girl or a boy.

God does not make mistakes.

Girl body parts
are not the
same as boy
body parts.

God made boy
body parts for
boys and girl
body parts for
girls.

HOW ARE YOU?

If the doctor
says I can be a
boy, I will say,
"No, God made
me a girl!"

I will celebrate being a girl no matter what anyone says.

When I look in the mirror, I see a blessing from God.

(Psalms 139:14)

As I grow, I will not let
others put limits on me.

I will do what I love and
have joy in my heart.

If I want to.......

I can play with airplanes, trucks, and soccer balls.

I can play with stuffed toys.

I can play with baby dolls too.

I can dance.

I can jump rope.

I can play vollyball.

I can play tennis.

I can play golf.

I can do martial arts.

I can play
softball.

I can play basketball.

I can ride a skateboard.

I can climb high mountains and be brave.

I don't have to be afraid because I believe in myself and God will help me.

As long as I am willing, I will be exactly what God created me to be.

I can play
the piano or
the flute and
make
beautiful
music.

I can play the violin,
cello, drums, or any
other instrument I
like.

I can be a
cheerleader
or twirl
the baton.

I can swim for fun or
for a swim team.

I can run for fun or
for a track team.

I can play with girls or boys if I choose to.

I can be friends with whomever I want as long as they are nice to me and I am nice to them.

I can garden and
work on a farm if
that is what I like
to do.

I can be a bird watcher or an explorer if I love being outside in nature.

I will remember
I am in the
world but not
of this world.
(Romans 12:2)

I will use the talents
God gave me to help
and bless others.

I can make a
difference.

I will not allow people at
school to tell me I can be a
boy. I will stand my ground
and rebuke the devil.

I will only read books that God would approve.
I will not look at grown up stuff or bad pictures.
LIBRARY

I will not listen to people on TV that tell
me I can choose to be a girl or a boy.

I am what God made me to be.
I am a girl!

I will only watch what
God would approve.

When I am on my tablet or computer, I will tell an adult if I see men dressed up as ladies and ladies acting like men.

If I see girls kissing girls or boys kissing boys I will turn away and say "I rebuke you devil!"

I can be a
chef or open
my own
restaurant.

I can feel happy or even sad sometimes.

No matter how sad I feel, I
won't blame it on being a girl.

Being a girl doesn't mean I can only wear dresses,

but when I grow up, I will not dress like a man.
(Deuteronomy 22:5)

I am beautiful no matter what style I choose to wear.

I am an amazing girl that will grow up to be
a strong, caring woman who loves herself.
(Philippians 4:13)

I will always remember that
rainbows belong to God.

They represent His promise to the world.
(Genesis 9:12-17)

Rainbows do not give
me permission to
disobey the word of God.

If someone tells me I
am a boy, I will say
"I rebuke you devil!"

TRUTH

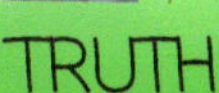

LIES

I am a girl, proud and strong!

I am not a he, we, us, or they. I am a HER or SHE.

I will NEVER be a HE nor a HIM because I am not a boy.

WORD OF GOD

Psalm 139:14 ESV

"I praise you, for I am fearfully and wonderfully made. Wonderful are your works; my soul knows it very well."

Romans 12:2 ESV

"Do not be conformed to this world, but be transformed by the renewal of your mind, that by testing you may discern what is the will of God, what is good and acceptable and perfect."

Philippians 4:13 ESV

"I can do all things through him who strengthens me."

Psalm 127:3 ESV

"Behold, children are a heritage from the Lord, the fruit of the womb a reward."

Matthew 19:14 ESV

"but Jesus said, "Let the little children come to me and do not hinder them, for to such belongs the kingdom of heaven."

Numbers 23:19 ESV

"God is not man, that he should lie, or a son of man, that he should change his mind. Has he said, and will he not do it? Or has he spoken, and will he not fulfill it?"

Deuteronomy 22::5 ESV

"A woman shall not wear a man's garment, nor shall a man put on a woman's cloak, for whoever does these things is an abomination to the Lord your God."

WORD OF GOD

Genesis 9: 11-17 ESV
"I establish my covenant with you, that never again shall all flesh be cut off by the waters of the flood, and never again shall there be a flood to destroy the earth." 12) And God said, "This is the sign of the covenant that I make between me and you and every living creature that is with you, for all future generations: 13) I have set my bow in the cloud, and it shall be a sign of the covenant between me and the earth. 14) When I bring clouds over the earth and the bow is seen in the clouds, 15) I will remember my covenant that is between me and you and every living creature of all flesh. And the waters shall never again become a flood to destroy all flesh. 16) When the bow is in the clouds, I will see it and remember the everlasting covenant between God and every living creature of all flesh that is on the earth." 17) God said to Noah, "This is the sign of the covenant that I have established between me and all flesh that is on the earth."

Genesis 5:2 ESV
"Male and female he created them, and he blessed them and named them Man when they were created."

Genesis 1:27 ESV
"So God created man in his own image, in the image of God he created him; male and female he created them."